Cambridge **Discovery Education**™
▶ **INTERACTIVE READERS**

Series editor: Bob Hastings

SHOOT TO KILL
WHY WE HUNT

A1⁺

Kathryn O'Dell

CAMBRIDGE
UNIVERSITY PRESS

DISCOVERY
EDUCATION™

Cambridge University Press
Cambridge, New York, Melbourne, Madrid, Cape Town,
Singapore, São Paulo, Delhi, Mexico City

Cambridge University Press
32 Avenue of the Americas, New York, NY 10013-2473, USA

www.cambridge.org
Information on this title: www.cambridge.org/9781107622531

First published 2014

Printed in Hong Kong, China, by Golden Cup Printing Company Limited

A catalog record for this publication is available from the British Library.

Library of Congress Cataloging-in-Publication Data

O'Dell, Kathryn.
  Shoot to kill : why we hunt / Kathryn O'Dell.
    pages cm. -- (Cambridge discovery interactive readers)
  ISBN 978-1-107-62253-1 (pbk. : alk. paper)
1. Hunting--Juvenile literature. 2. English language--Textbooks for foreign speakers. 3. Readers
(Elementary) I. Title.

SK35.5.O35 2014
639'.1071--dc23

                    2013016504

ISBN 978-1-107-62253-1

Additional resources for this publication at www.cambridge.org

Layout services, art direction, book design, and photo research: Q2ABillSMITH GROUP
Editorial services: Hyphen S.A.
Audio production: CityVox, New York
Video production: Q2ABillSMITH GROUP

Contents

Before You Read:
Get Ready!

There are many different reasons people hunt animals. You are going to read about many different kinds of hunting in this book.

Words to Know

Read the texts. Then complete the sentences with the correct highlighted words.

A Dangerous Animal at the Clinton Zoo!

A tiger attacks a boy at a zoo. The tiger hurts the boy, and he has to go to the hospital. The boy's mother says, "This zoo is dangerous. Children can get too close to the animals. My son almost died. I want to know the reason why.

People Help Endangered Tigers

In the 1900s, there were over 100,000 wild tigers in the world. Today, there are no more than 4,000. They are endangered. It is possible that, very soon, there won't be any wild tigers in the world. People must protect them. Many groups help tigers.

1 If an animal is _____ , it is possible that soon there aren't going to be any living in the world.

2 If an animal is _____ , it does not live where people live.

3 Someone who _____ somebody makes them feel pain.

4 Something _____ is not safe.

5 Someone who _____ tries to hurt somebody.

6 To _____ is to make something or somebody safe.

7 When you ask "Why?", you want to find the _____ for something.

Words to Know

Read the definitions. Then complete the sentences with the correct highlighted words.

capture: catch something

hunt: make wild animals die, or to look for wild animals

kill: make something die

record: write down things that are important or useful, or put them on a computer

relocate: put something in a new place

1 Some people _____ a raccoon.

2 People _____ how long a snake is.

3 People sometimes hit animals with their cars and _____ them.

4 People _____ birds from a zoo to a park.

5 Many people _____ animals. They want to kill them and eat them.

?

APPLY

What wild animals do you know? Are they dangerous? Are they endangered?

CHAPTER 1

Hunting

A deer

WHAT DO YOU THINK OF WHEN YOU THINK OF HUNTING?

Meet Wayne Douglas. He is a hunter. He hunts deer every year during hunting season.[1] After he **kills** deer, he cleans them. He and his family eat the deer meat all year. Maybe you think of someone like Wayne when you think of hunting.

Paul and Sue Rogers are on vacation in Costa Rica. They catch a lot of fish, but they don't eat them. For them, fishing is fun. They fish for sport.

Some people hunt animals for money. They kill them and **sell** parts of their bodies.

[1] **hunting season:** a time of year when hunters can hunt wild animals

Fishing on the beach

Jeff Corwin hunts alligators to help them.

Other people hunt animals, but they don't kill them. They study the animals to help people or to help the animals. Jeff Corwin, for example, **captures** animals and studies them. He gets information[2] about them. Later, he uses this information to help the animals.

People hunt for food, but they also hunt for other reasons. They hunt for sport. They hunt for fun. They hunt for money. They hunt to help people. And sometimes they hunt animals to help the animals.

People have many reasons to hunt. They also have many opinions[3] about hunting.

[2]**information:** things that are useful or important to know about somebody or something
[3]**opinion:** what you think about something or somebody

?

EVALUATE

What do you think about hunting for fun? What do you think about hunting for food?

7

A white fox

CHAPTER 2

Helping People

An actress[4] walks into a movie theater. She's wearing a fox coat. An angry person puts red paint on her. The person thinks it is wrong to wear **fur**. Many others have the same feelings.

In the past, people used every part of an animal. We ate the meat and used the fur for clothes. Today, people use animal fur for coats, but we often do not use all of the animal. We capture and kill some **wild** animals only for their fur.

....

[4]**actress:** a woman in a movie or on TV

Sometimes, we capture wild animals, but we do not kill them. We keep them as pets.

Most people think that birds and cats are good pets. How about monkeys and tigers? Do they make good pets? Some people buy wild animals in pet stores. Other people get them from the **wild**, and they take them home. Sometimes, these animals are **endangered**.

It is illegal[5] in many places to have a wild animal for a pet. Why? First, because it is dangerous. Wild animals can attack people. Also, it is not good for the animal. Many wild animals get sick out of the wild.

....

[5]**illegal:** something you cannot do because it is not OK to do

A pet monkey

People also capture wild animals to use them for medical research.[6] One example is snakes.

Researchers capture snakes and take their venom. Then they use the venom to make a drug.[7] Doctors give this drug to people when a snake **bites** them.

Years ago, many people died from snakebites. In the US today, only about five people die from snakebites every year. Medical research helped make snakebites less dangerous.

Medical research uses animals, and those animals sometimes get sick or die. For this reason, some people think medical research is **cruel**. Today, researchers mostly use mice – over 25,000,000 (25 million) mice every year!

[6]**medical research:** the study of a subject to help sick people get better
[7]**drug:** something sick people eat or drink to make them better

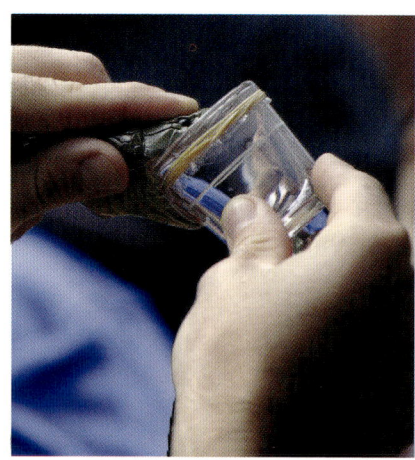

A researcher takes the venom from a snake.

Researchers often use mice for their tests on new drugs.

Wild hogs are a problem in Texas.

Hunting helps people in other ways.[8] A farmer in Texas has a problem: wild hogs. These animals are killing his farm animals. They are eating his food. He is worried they are going to attack his children. He calls Jerry Campbell. Jerry and his family are hog hunters. They hunt wild hogs to **protect** people.

Hunters sometimes kill dangerous animals when they get too close to people. In Texas, there are about one million wild hogs. They live very close to people. Farmers lose about $50 million a year because of the hogs. Hunters kill the hogs to help the farmers.

[8]**way:** how you do something

Video Quest

Grizzly Bears in Canada

Watch this video about a town in Alaska with a bear problem. What happens to the bears?

CHAPTER 3

Helping Animals

DOES HUNTING HELP ANIMALS?

Can hunting be good for animals? Yes, it can! Hunting can help animals in many ways.

With no hunting, some groups of animals get too big. This is a problem for all of the animals in the group. Take deer, for example. In some places, there are too many deer. There is not enough food for all of the deer. They are hungry. Many deer die, slowly and painfully.[9] Others leave their homes to find food. They go into cities where cars hit and kill them.

Hunters kill some of the deer to stop the number of animals from getting too big. Many people feel it is less cruel for the deer to die like this.

....

[9]**painfully:** in a way that hurts

Marcos and Carol are whale hunters. They capture a whale, but they don't kill it. They put a small computer on the whale. It records what the whale does. It shows where the whale goes. Marcos and Carol learn about whales from the information. Then they try to help other whales.

Many people hunt animals to study them. They do not kill the animals. They capture them and record information about them. This helps people understand the problems of a group of animals. Later, people use this information to help the animals.

A computer records information about the whale.

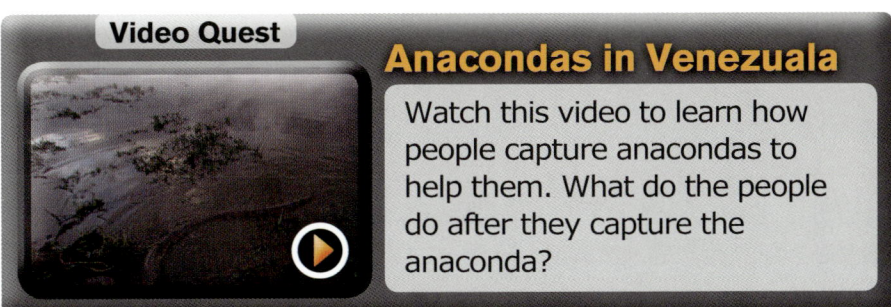

Video Quest

Anacondas in Venezuala

Watch this video to learn how people capture anacondas to help them. What do the people do after they capture the anaconda?

A bear in a town

Other people capture animals to **relocate** them. Karen Parsons lives in New Jersey. One day, she saw a bear in her yard. She was worried. She didn't want it to attack her or her children. She called an animal control center.[10] They captured the bear and took it back to its home.

People often relocate an animal when it leaves its home and goes into a city. People at an animal control center take the animal back to its home. If this is not possible, they take it to a zoo. This protects people and the animal.

---

[10]**animal control center:** a place where wild animals can be safe

Sometimes people relocate groups of animals. This can help endangered animals. For example, the Florida panther was endangered. These panthers only lived in one part of Florida in the United States. There were only about 100 of them living in the wild.

People found safe places for the panthers to live in other parts of Florida and Georgia. They captured some of the panthers and relocated them to these places. There are going to be about 250 panthers in each new place in a few years.

A Florida panther

? ANALYZE

How do people choose a new home for animals? What things do they think about?

CHAPTER 4

Poaching

POACHING IS A PROBLEM IN MANY COUNTRIES.

In many places, there are some times of the year when it is OK for people to hunt wild animals and some times when it is illegal. Poaching is hunting and killing wild animals when it is illegal.

For example, in the United States there is a deer season. This is the time of year when it is OK, or legal, to hunt deer. It is illegal to hunt deer at other times. This protects the deer, but it also helps hunters. For example, it is illegal to hunt deer when babies are with their mothers. If a hunter kills the mother, the baby dies, too. So next year, there aren't so many deer, and that's not good for hunters.

Poachers can sell this animal's horns.

Poachers often kill endangered animals. Why? For money. Some people pay a lot of money for endangered animals – for example, $20,000 for the horns of a bighorn sheep. If poaching doesn't stop, some animals are going to disappear.[11] In the early 1800s, there were over 1,500,000 bighorn sheep in North America. Today, there are fewer than 70,000.

Some people think that poachers are not hunters. Hunters kill animals for good reasons, but poachers do not.

[11] **disappear:** not live in any place in the world

Video Quest

Poaching in Cambodia

Watch this video to learn about endangered animals in Cambodia. Which ones do poachers want to capture?

CHAPTER 5

Hunting Parks

HUNTING PARKS ARE LIKE ZOOS FOR HUNTERS. BUT IS THAT A GOOD THING OR A BAD THING?

A hunter can pay money to hunt wild animals in a hunting park. Think about the wild hog problem in Texas. Many wild hogs live in Texas, but they do not live in New York State. But there is a hunting park with many wild hogs in New York State. People brought wild hogs to the park so others can hunt them.

There are many hunting parks in the world. People go to these parks for "hunting vacations." Some hunting parks have zoo animals like rhinoceroses, tigers, and zebras. Hunters pay a lot of money to hunt these wild animals.

But some people think hunting in hunting parks is not right. The animals have no place to go. They can't escape[12] from the hunters. People feel this is cruel to the animals.

There can be problems with hunting parks, too. For example, in New York State, some of the wild hogs got out of the park.

Others think there is nothing wrong with hunting parks. They are legal, and hunters can use their money in any way they want.

There are benefits[13] to hunting parks, too. When zoos have too many animals or older animals, they can sell them to a hunting park. The zoos get money to make the zoo better. They can also use the money for medical research to help all animals.

[12]**escape:** get away, leave a place
[13]**benefit:** something good; it helps you

Hunters pay a lot of money to hunt rhinoceroses and zebras.

What Do You Think?

IN THIS BOOK YOU READ ABOUT MANY DIFFERENT KINDS OF HUNTING. AND YOU SAW THAT PEOPLE HAVE DIFFERENT OPINIONS ABOUT HUNTING.

1. Choose one of the topics from the charts.

2. Read the part of the chapter about the topic again.

3. What do you think? Give reasons for your opinion.

Topic	Opinion 1	Opinion 2
People kill animals and use their fur for coats. (Chapter 2, p. 8)	People wore fur coats in the past. It is not wrong to use fur for coats.	Some people kill animals only for their fur. It is cruel to kill an animal to have a fur coat.
People use animals for medical research. (Chapter 2, p. 10)	This research helps people. It can stop people from dying.	It is not right to use animals to help people in this way. There are other kinds of research to help people.
People kill animals or they relocate them when they come into cities. (Chapter 2, p. 11 and Chapter 3, pp. 14–15)	It's dangerous for wild animals to be near people. People need to kill the animals to protect their children.	People don't have to kill the animals. They can relocate them to their homes or zoos.
People kill animals in hunting parks. (Chapter 5, pp. 18–19)	It's OK to kill animals in hunting parks. The money can help other animals in zoos.	It is cruel to kill animals in hunting parks. The animals aren't really wild, and they have no place to go.

After You Read

Read the sentences and choose Ⓐ (True) or Ⓑ (False).

1 Wild animals always make good pets.
- Ⓐ True
- Ⓑ False

2 Today, medical researchers mostly use mice.
- Ⓐ True
- Ⓑ False

3 Hunting never helps animals.
- Ⓐ True
- Ⓑ False

4 Hunters capture whales to relocate them.
- Ⓐ True
- Ⓑ False

5 Wild hogs are a problem in Texas.
- Ⓐ True
- Ⓑ False

6 Poachers don't kill endangered animals.
- Ⓐ True
- Ⓑ False

7 Poachers can make a lot of money.
- Ⓐ True
- Ⓑ False

8 Some hunting parks use zoo animals.
- Ⓐ True
- Ⓑ False

About You

Rate the sentences with your own opinion.
1 = always OK, 2 = sometimes OK, 3 = never OK.
Challenge: Choose one of the sentences. Give your opinion. Give reasons for your opinion.

1 _____ A hunter kills a wild animal for food.

2 _____ An animal attacks a person. A hunter kills the dangerous animal.

3 _____ A person kills an endangered animal.

4 _____ A hunter kills an animal at a hunting park.

5 _____ A person captures an animal and records information about it.

6 _____ A person kills an animal and uses its fur for a coat.

7 _____ A person uses an animal for medical research.

Complete the Ad

Choose the correct words to complete the ad about saving tigers.

Help the Tigers!

We need you to help us
1 _____ (protect/kill) tigers.

Did You Know?

- There are only about 3,200 **2** _____ (wild/pet) tigers in the world today.

- People **3** _____ (protect/hunt) and kill tigers. It is illegal!

- Our group helps many tigers. We **4** _____ (record/relocate) tigers to safe places.

Give a little money to help **5** _____ (an endangered/a dangerous) tiger today!

Answer Key

Words to Know, page 4

1 endangered **2** wild **3** hurts **4** dangerous **5** attacks
6 protect **7** reason

Words to Know, page 5

1 capture **2** record **3** kill **4** relocate **5** hunt

Apply, page 5

Answers will vary.

Evaluate, page 7

Answers will vary.

Video Quest, page 11

Hunters hunt the bears to protect people.

Video Quest, page 13

They get information about the anacondas to help
them understand the anacondas. Then, they return the
anacondas where they found them.

Analyze, page 15

Answers will vary.

Video Quest, page 17

Poachers want elephants, bears, and tigers. They also want
wild cats called civits.

True or False, page 22

1 B **2** A **3** B **4** B **5** A **6** B **7** A **8** A

About You, page 22

Answers will vary.

Complete the Ad, page 23

1 protect **2** wild **3** hunt **4** relocate **5** an endangered